Gill and Bill Are Full

By Clem King

Bill and Gill love
to have snacks.
They pull moss and kelp
from the rocks.

Bill spots some red kelp on a tall rock wall.

"I will swim to get that red kelp!" said Bill.

"We do not go to that wall!" said Gill.

"But that bit is full of kelp!" said Bill.

“Do you think a troll is down there?” Bill scoffed.

"No, but a big fish could get you!" called Gill.

Bill went stiff.

"I did not think of that at all!" said Bill.

Gill pulled Bill into a hug.

"I do not want a big fish to get you!" said Gill.

Gill and Bill had a big snack.

“I am so **full**!” said Gill.

“I am too!” said Bill.

CHECKING FOR MEANING

1. What do Bill and Gill eat besides moss? *(Literal)*
2. What sort of kelp does Bill spot? *(Literal)*
3. Which fish do you think is more cautious, Gill or Bill? Why? *(Inferential)*

EXTENDING VOCABULARY

pull	Read the word *pull*. What does it mean if you pull on something? What word means the opposite of *pull*?
bliss	Bill describes moss as *bliss*. What does this mean? When else might you feel bliss? What words do you know that have a similar meaning to *bliss*?
troll	What is a troll? Is it likely that a troll would live in the sea?

MOVING BEYOND THE TEXT

1. What are some other creatures that live in the sea?
2. How can we take care of the sea to keep it healthy for the animals that live in it?
3. Bill and Gill like to eat plants. What kinds of plants do you like to eat?
4. Gill was a great friend. In what ways are you a good friend?

SPEED SOUNDS

PRACTICE WORDS

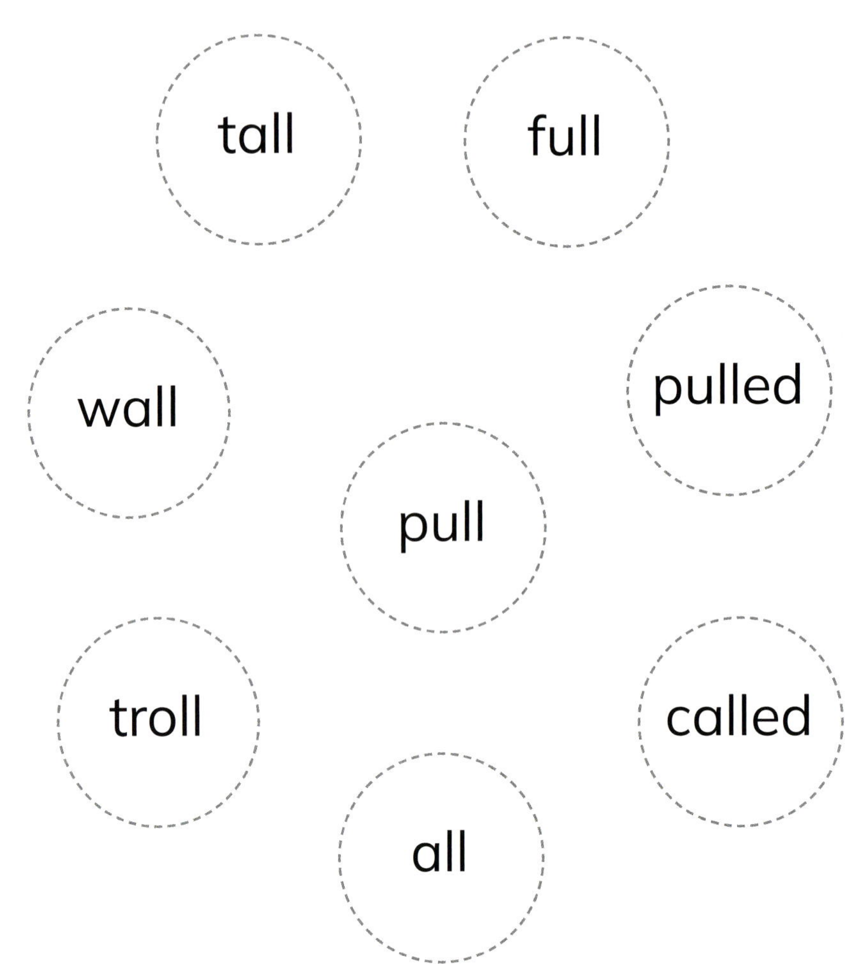